Why does the Pope wear white?

CTS Children's Books

Contents

Text by: Pierpaolo Finaldi

Illustrations by: Ettore & Mattia Finaldi

Photographs © Stefano Spaziani except Page 5: DOMENICO STINELLIS/AP/Press Association Images, Page 11: © Alinari Archives/CORBIS, Page 17: © Franco Origlia/Getty Images News, Page 21: © ETTORE FERRARI /epa/Corbis, Page 23: © Alessandra Benedetti/Corbis

Questions: Special thanks go to Miss Collins and all the children of Year 5 in Holy Cross School, Catford, London.

Why does the Pope wear white?: Published 2010 by the Incorporated Catholic Truth Society, 40-46 Harleyford Road, London SE11 5AY. Tel: 020 7640 0042; Fax: 020 7640 0046; www.cts-online.org.uk. Copyright © 2010 The Incorporated Catholic Truth Society.

ISBN: 978 1 86082 673 3   CTS Code CH 25

'Viva il Papa!'
- Long Live the Pope!

The Pope lives in the Vatican which is in Rome, the capital of Italy. In Italy every child calls his Dad, Papa. The Pope is also called 'il Papa' because he is like a Dad for every Catholic. He cares for all of us, and like every good Dad he doesn't always say what we want to hear but he tells us what we need to do to be happy.

The Pope says Mass every morning and spends a long time praying every day. He stays close to God and shows us how we can stay close to God as well.

This book was written answering questions asked by the children of Year 5 in Holy Cross School in Catford, South East London while they prepared for the visit of Pope Benedict the XVI to Britain in 2010.

When did Pope Benedict become Pope?

John Paul II was a great Pope and looked after the Church for over 25 years. He had travelled to most countries in the world to encourage the Catholics there to be holy. He worked hard for people in Eastern Europe to be free to worship God and had prayed together with people of every other religion for peace in the world. He died at the grand old age of 85, everybody was very sad but also excited to see who would be chosen to carry on his work.

All the Cardinals in the world gathered together in Rome and in the Sistine chapel they tried to understand who God wanted to lead the Church.

Each Cardinal wrote the name of the man they thought would be holy and lead all the Catholics in the world towards heaven. Great crowds waited for their decision in St Peter's square.

When the votes were counted if there was not a clear winner the votes were burned together with some damp straw and all the crowds saw black smoke coming from a chimney high above the square. After only one day most of the Cardinals voted for a man called Joseph Ratzinger. They burned the votes without any straw and white smoke came out. Everybody cheered because this meant that God had given the Church a new leader.

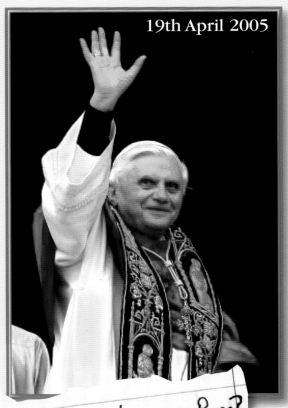

19th April 2005

When did Pope Benedict become Pope?

Why does the Pope choose a new name?

When somebody becomes Pope he starts a new life and most Popes have chosen a new name as well. They can choose a name to remember a saint or another Pope who they liked. Cardinal Joseph Ratzinger became Pope and he chose the name Benedict hoping to carry on the work of those who had that name in the past. He was the sixteenth Pope to choose the name Benedict.

St Benedict was a famous saint from Italy who lived 1500 years ago. He was the first monk in Europe and together with his followers, built monasteries where people lived together, prayed together and worked and studied together. His monasteries helped people to live holy lives and spread the light of Jesus through the whole of Europe.

Pope Benedict hoped that he would also bring the light of Jesus to many people in Europe who had forgotten him. Pope Benedict XV who was the last Pope who had chosen that name had also worked hard for peace during the First World War and Pope Benedict wanted to work just as hard for peace in our world.

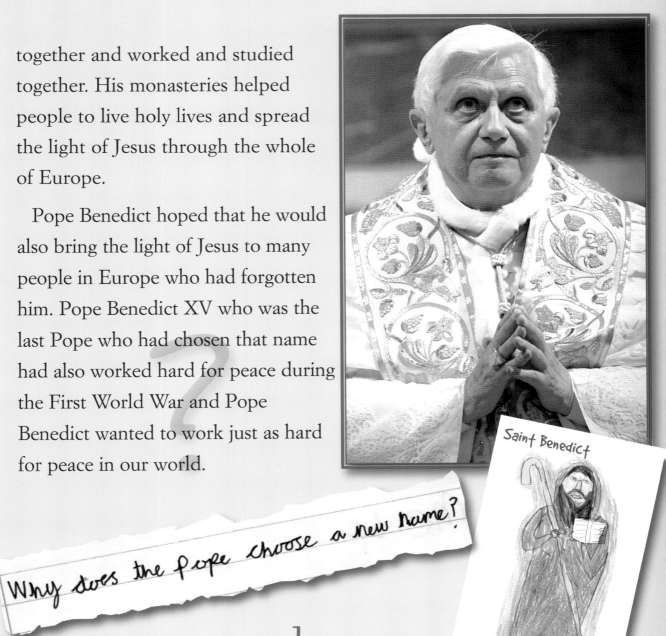

Saint Benedict

Why does the Pope choose a new name?

Why does the Pope wear white?

The Pope wears a beautiful long tunic called a 'soutane' (pronounced soo-tan) and a short cape over his shoulders called a 'mozzetta' (pronounced mot-set-a). Priests wear black and bishops wear purple and Cardinals wear red but only the Pope wears white, and he really stands out from the crowd!

For almost 1500 years, Popes used to wear red or purple, but then a monk who was a follower of St Dominic became Pope Pius the Fifth (or V in Roman numerals). He had always worn the white tunic or habit which Dominicans wear. So when he became

Pope he decided to continue wearing white. Ever since then all the Popes have worn white.

Every Christian including you and I wore something white when we were baptised. It shows that our sins have been washed away by the water of baptism and that we are clean. The Pope shows all the world he is a Christian by wearing white.

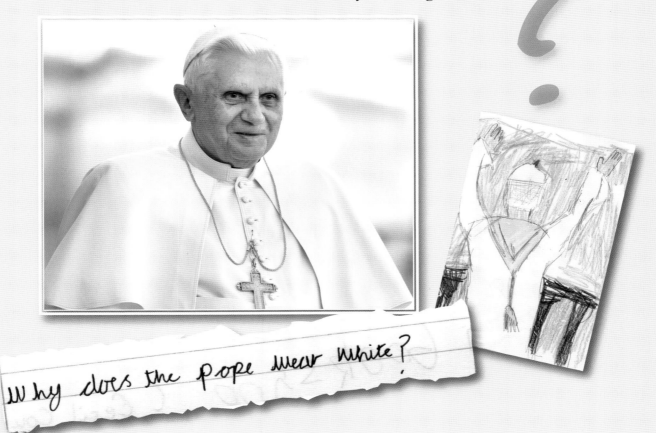

Why does the Pope wear white?

Why does the Pope live in Rome?

The Pope actually lives in the Vatican which is the smallest country in the world. It has only 800 inhabitants and is located in the city of Rome in Italy. After Jesus died and rose again in Jerusalem, the Apostles began to spread the Gospel around the rest of the Roman empire and beyond. Rome was the biggest and most important city in the world and there were lots of people there who needed to hear the Good News. St Peter went to Rome and preached the Gospel to everyone who would listen. He looked after all the Christians there and was the first Bishop of Rome. The Emperor however, was afraid of the Christians and had Peter crucified upside down. He is buried in St Peter's Basilica (or Church). But his death was not in vain, within a few hundred years, the whole of Rome was Christian, including the Emperor, and the Bishops of Rome who came after St Peter have been the leaders of the Church ever since all the way up to our Pope today.

Why does the pope live in Rome?

Why does the Pope wear a special ring?

The Pope wears a gold ring which is called the fisherman's ring. It is engraved with an image of St Peter, who was the first Pope, fishing from his boat. This reminds the Pope that he is a fisher of men just like St Peter.

In the old days the ring was pushed into warm wax which was dripped onto the bottom of important documents. It meant that whatever was on the document had been said by the Pope himself and had to be done.

Today every Bishop wears a ring and the Pope is the Bishop of Rome. The ring is a bit like a wedding ring and symbolizes that the Pope will look after his church as though it was his wife and that he will be faithful to it and love it until the day he dies.

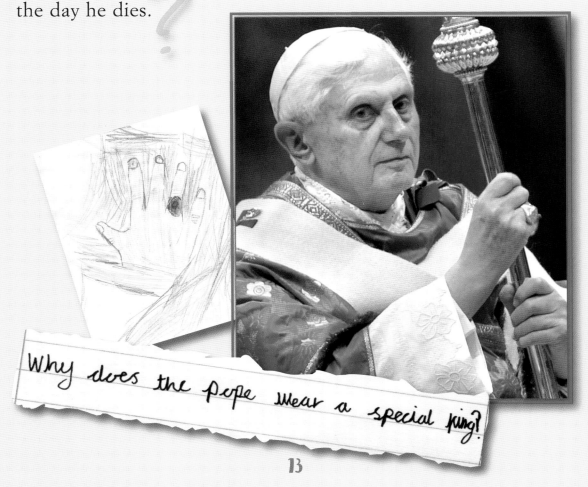

Why does the pope wear a special ring?

Why does the Pope carry a big cross and wear a funny hat?

When Jesus asked St Peter to look after the Church, he said: "Peter do you love me? Then feed my sheep." Jesus wanted Peter, who was the first Pope, to look after all Christians like a shepherd, protecting them and feeding them. Shepherds always carry a staff which helps them to walk ahead of the flock and with which they can protect their sheep. Every bishop carries a staff called a crozier to show that they are the shepherds of their flock but only the Pope carries one with a cross on it.

14

Jesus loved us all so much that he gave his life for us on the cross to take away our sins. The Pope's first job is to show the whole world how much Jesus loved every human being and there is no better way to do that, than to show Jesus on the cross with his arms opened wide, welcoming everyone.

The Pope's hat is called a mitre. Its shape reminds us of the tongues of fire which appeared on the heads of the apostles. It tells us that the Pope and all the Bishops have been given the Holy Spirit to help them.

Why does the Pope carry a big cross and wear a funny hat?

Does the Pope have anyone to help him?

When St Peter wasn't sure what do, he talked about it with the other disciples and then took a decision. The Pope also has many helpers he can count on. There are about 120 Cardinals who are chosen because of their holy lives and because of all the good they have done in their work as priests and bishops; these are the Pope's closest advisers. Then there are the Bishops from around the world who visit the Pope in Rome and tell him about what is happening in their countries and what is needed there and ask for his advice.

The Bishops pass on what the Pope says to the priests in their churches all around the world. If you listen carefully the priest mentions the Pope and the bishop every time you go to Mass and prays for them. Every Catholic including you and me can help the Pope by praying for him and for his intentions which are published every month on the internet.

Does the pope have anyone to help him?

Why can't a woman be Pope?

When Jesus was on earth he had many followers including lots of women. He chose twelve apostles to do special jobs like baptise people and forgive sins. They were all men and the jobs that they did are done today by priests who are also men. He chose one of those men, Peter, to be the leader of the Church and to look after it, and just as Jesus chose from those twelve apostles, so the Pope is chosen from among the men who are their successors today.

Jesus also had special followers who were women and gave them some of the most important tasks of all. When Jesus rose from the dead the news was given first to a woman, Mary of Magdala. She was the one who told the apostles and the world about the greatest event in history.

St. Peter

Why can't a woman be Pope?

Does the Pope travel a lot?

Pope John Paul II visited 129 countries and travelled over 700,000 miles which is further than going to the moon and back.

Pope Benedict has also been to many different countries. The Pope does not travel because he likes it, but because one of his most important jobs is to encourage Catholics to be holy. The Pope travels to meet people of different nationalities, or to meet young people or to speak to kings, queens and presidents to encourage them to make good decisions.

Sometimes the Pope will go on a pilgrimage to pray at a shrine like Lourdes or to bless a special place, like a new Cathedral, or to declare that somebody is officially a hero of the Church: a blessed or a saint, like Cardinal John Henry Newman.

Does the pope travel a lot?

How does the Pope make people Saints?

There are many saints already in heaven. Some are famous and well known and have churches named after them and beautiful paintings made of them. Others lived their whole life for Jesus or maybe even died for him without anyone else knowing. You may know a saint yourself; a relative, a friend or a priest or nun who loves God more than anything else!

If someone has been especially brave or holy during their life or death, the Church investigates whether we can be sure that they are in heaven. One way to find out is if people pray to God

22

for a miracle through that person and the miracle happens then we can be sure that they are with God.

This happened with an English man called John Henry Newman, he was a great writer who wrote books and poems about Jesus and the Church. An American man was healed by praying to him and Pope Benedict proclaimed that he could be called Blessed John Henry Newman. Pope Benedict made Fr Damien a Saint as well. He had looked after lepers for most of his life when no one else would.

Maybe one day a Pope will make you a Saint!

Father Damien

How does the Pope make people saints?

CTS Children's Books

The Beautiful Story of Jesus, by Maïte Roche (CTS Code CH 13)

The Beautiful Story of the Bible, by Maïte Roche (CTS Code CH 27)

Benedict & Chico, by Jeanne Perego (CTS Code CH 12)

The Bible for little children, by Maïte Roche (CTS Code CH 2)

First prayers for little children, by Maïte Roche (CTS Code CH 5)

Friendship with Jesus, by Amy Welborn (CTS Code CH 26)

Getting to know God, by Christine Pedotti (CTS Code CH 9)

The Gospel for little children, by Maïte Roche (CTS Code CH 1)

Max & Benedict, by Jeanne Perego (CTS Code CH 24)

The most beautiful Christmas Story, by Maïte Roche (CTS Code CH 8)

My Little Missal, by Maïte Roche (CTS Code CH 20)

Prayers around the Crib, by Juliette Levivier (CTS Code CH 7)

Praying at Mass, by Juliette Levivier (CTS Code CH 11)

Praying with Mary, by Juliette Levivier (CTS Code CH 14)

Praying with the Holy Spirit, by Juliette Levivier (CTS Code CH 15)

Praying with the first Christians, by Juliette Levivier (CTS Code CH 10)

Praying with the Friends of Jesus, by Juliette Levivier (CTS Code CH 6)

The Rosary, by Juliette Levivier (CTS Code CH 3)

Saint Anthony of Padua, by Silvia Vecchini (CTS Code CH 16)

Saint Francis of Assisi, by Silvia Vecchini (CTS Code CH 17)

Saint John Mary Vianney, by Silvia Vecchini (CTS Code CH 28)

Saint Lucy, by Silvia Vecchini (CTS Code CH 19)

Saint Martin, by Silvia Vecchini (CTS Code CH 29)

Saint Paul, by Silvia Vecchini (CTS Code CH 22)

Saint Rita of Cascia, by Silvia Vecchini (CTS Code CH 18)

Saint Thérèse of Lisieux, by Silvia Vecchini (CTS Code CH 23)

The Way of the Cross, by Juliette Levivier (CTS Code CH 4)

Why does the Pope wear white?, by Pierpaolo Finaldi (CTS Code CH 25)